DEBATING CATHOLICISM: BOOK 2

High Desert Showdown

Karl Keating

RASSELAS
HOUSE

Published by Rasselas House
El Cajon, California
RasselasHouse.com

Cover design by EbookLaunch.com
Formatting by PolgarusStudio.com

ISBN 978-1-942596-25-7 Paperback
ISBN 978-1-942596-24-0 Ebook

Contents

Introduction

For decades U.S. Route 395 was the only north-south highway in eastern California. It still is. There have been few changes to the route or to the towns along it. The largest town is Ridgecrest, population 28,000. It has the distinction of being within a two-hour drive of the highest and lowest points in the contiguous U.S., Mt. Whitney (14,505 feet) and Badwater Basin in Death Valley (282 feet below sea level). Ridgecrest is as large as it is chiefly because it is home to Naval Air Weapons Station China Lake. The town's population is a cross-section of America: urban and rural, well educated and not, financially secure and financially precarious. It displays much of the panoply of American Christianity.

One day I received a plea from Catholics who lived in Ridgecrest. Would I come to town to debate a Fundamentalist minister, the pastor of Watchman Baptist Church, who was riling the local populace? Townsfolk were beginning to turn against one another. The Catholics were at wit's end. None of them felt equipped to deal with the man, who was inflaming emotions in a way not seen before. Sure, I said. I had been wanting to visit the high desert again, and this would be a good excuse.

I was asked to begin with a lecture given at the military base's chapel the evening before the debate. In the lecture I spoke about the Bible as understood by the Catholic Church, how it is the pre-eminently Catholic book, how the Church decided upon its canon, and how it ought to be interpreted by Catholics and non-Catholics alike. I had the leisure of making the positive case for the Catholic Church, anticipating objections without having to discuss them directly.

I explained that the Bible isn't so much the book of the individual Christian but the book of the Christian Church. It—particularly the New Testament—was composed by Churchmen, and it was the Church that decided that the Bible's constituent books were inspired and that other books claiming inspiration were not. It was the Church that was given authority by Christ to interpret the Bible, I said, and it was necessary that there be a reliable and consistent—even infallible—interpreter, as demonstrated sufficiently in our own time when even people of the same denomination elicit contradictory understandings from the sacred text. If Baptists often enough disagree among themselves, and if they disagree with other Protestants on many matters, doctrinal and procedural, and with Catholics on even a greater number—how can a Christian know for certain what the Bible means if he is left to his own devices?

The evening lecture was the preparatory event. The main event was the next day's debate, the topic of which was "What Is the Truth about the Catholic Church?" The debate was held on the campus of Cerro Coso Community College, a small school serving students who live within a huge district of 18,000 square miles. Many of Pastor Jim Blackburn's congregants were in the audience. He had prepped them over the preceding weeks. They expected fireworks from him, but apparently many of them got more than they could deal with. So bitter was he toward the Catholic Church during our exchange that he lost much of his following over the following days—but not, apparently, his animosity. After I departed Ridgecrest he volunteered to write a column for a neighboring town's newspaper. The editor happily gave him space, small-town newspapers always being in need of copy. The column turned out to be crassly anti-Catholic. Catholics living in the area asked the editor to yank the column. He refused, saying he liked Blackburn's opinions. The Catholics showed the column to the newspaper's advertisers, asking, "Is this the kind of newspaper you should be advertising in?" Most didn't think so, and they promptly removed their ads. A week later, Blackburn's column was gone. Not long after that so was his church, which was unable to survive with its reduced membership.

Whatever became of Blackburn I can't say. I lost track of him and sometimes have wondered where he went, whether he remained in ministry, whether his prejudices against Catholicism ever softened. I suppose not, based on probabilities. I have yet to meet a once-Catholic-now-anti-Catholic who developed a bit of a name for himself by attacking Rome and then realized that he had blundered grievously, repented, and returned to the Catholic Church. There must be some such, but I haven't met any. I have met any number of pew sitters who, originally Catholic, eventually returned to the faith of their upbringing, but professional anti-Catholics, those whose reputations were built on attacking "papistry"? No. If professional anti-Catholics who once had been Catholic rarely do an about-face, how much rarer must it be for professional anti-Catholics who had been brought up Fundamentalist and had imbibed confusions and fantasies about Catholicism from youth? Apples still don't fall far from their trees.

Jim Blackburn's church may not have survived the debate and his publishing escapade, but the ideas he expressed no doubt remained behind in Ridgecrest. People come and go while ideas, even bad ones, perdure. He was just another in the long parade of Fundamentalist preachers who found success—if only fleeting—in taking on the Church of Rome. He made anti-Catholicism his avocation, perhaps thinking thereby to attract an ever-increasing band of loyalists to his church. The attempt backfired, but not before he got off salvos that may have pleased as many as they irritated.

My opponent in this debate may have disappeared down the collective memory hole, but there remain thousands like him across the country, some shepherding small churches, others leading substantial ministries that boast presences online, on the air, and in print. There are not enough Catholic apologists even to begin a game of whack-a-mole. An anti-Catholic in one town might be countered successfully, but there remains another in the next town over. This is as true in urban as in rural areas. Most of the professional anti-Catholics I have dealt with over the years more likely might be called city slickers than country bumpkins, even if most of them sported—or at least affected—that Southern drawl commonly associated with Fundamentalist preachers, even those who never seem to have visited south of the Mason-Dixon Line.

I don't remember Jim Blackburn's voice. He may not have had the dulcet tones of Alabama, but his arguments were representative of an anti-Catholicism that may have become less common over the last few decades but that still has force and still attracts adherents by its assertiveness if not its cogency. But judge for yourself as you read the debate.

Notes on the Text

The following transcript has been edited for clarity and concision. I have taken the liberty of correcting grammatical errors and obvious misstatements, and I have removed those seemingly unavoidable hesitations and starts (ah's and um's and their cousins) that may not be particularly off-putting when spoken but seem to gouge the eyes when in print. The four debates in the series have been made roughly uniform in length. When given publicly, they ranged from two hours to an almost unendurable four hours, counting question-and-answer sessions. Each is now short enough to be read at a single sitting.

I have attempted to retain each speaker's best arguments, feeling no temptation to omit my opponents' most persuasive comments. (I think the Catholic position, however inadequately expressed by me, is match enough for any charge leveled against it.) I have omitted or truncated exchanges that were redundant or seemed unhelpful to the audiences. Also omitted have been audience questions that strayed too far from the topics of the debates or that were not true questions but attempted preaching sessions.

Looking back at my own arguments, particularly those made when on defense, I find places where I could have made a better reply. I have not gussied up my remarks. A reader may say, "But you could have said *this*!" My excuse must be that *this* didn't occur to me at that moment. Perhaps I was taken off guard. Perhaps my mind went blank. Perhaps I just didn't yet know the best answer and could offer only the second-best answer. What is presented here is verisimilitude. I can use a phrase from nineteenth-century German historian Leopold von Ranke. I have attempted to give the story "*wie es eigentlich gewesen*"—"how it really was."

And how it really is today. There is not a single anti-Catholic claim in these books that has fallen out of circulation. The claims have been around for lifetimes, and there is no likelihood that they ever will disappear completely, human nature and human obstinacy being what they are. I have tried to respond to the claims with candor and fairness. Whether I have succeeded is for readers to judge. Throughout the debates I kept in mind that "the truth shall set you free." I always have found searching for truth—and debating what is true—to be exhilarating. I hope you will too, as you read what follows, and I hope these pages bring solace and confidence to Catholics and intrigue and light to non-Catholics.

Debate Transcript
Karl Keating vs. Jim Blackburn

MODERATOR: We will begin with opening remarks of fifteen minutes by Rev. Blackburn.

BLACKBURN: Let me preface my statements. I'm trying to give you my heart a little bit, okay? I'm a man, and I'm subject to emotions. And as the moderator said, this is material that can get people riled. It can get them to speak very hotly, and I'm a person who can get speakin' hotly. But, please, if I should slip, I'll try not to, don't take it personally. I do not hate Catholics. I've spent 17 years of my life, my adult life, not as a child, 17 years of my adult life, in the Catholic Church. I do not like Catholicism. There is a difference between the teachings of the Church and the members of the Church, because I know what the teachings go to and what they have led to and where they will lead to, eventually.

Now, there are a number of reasons that you are gathered here today. Some of you are here in hopes of seeing your champion dispose of a Fundamentalist. Some of you are here hoping the Fundamentalist will dispose of the Catholic champion. Some of you are here just out of curiosity, and quite probably some of you are here to hear the truth, to discern what is the truth. There is only one truth. I'm sure it was a slip of words, last night when Mr. Keating made the statement that some things are truer and some things are less true. Of course, we know that's impossible. You either got to be true or you got to be false. You can't be truer or less true.

Another thing, I want to set the stage for this. Again, I apologize if I get a little strong in my words. I shook hands with Mr. Keating, but Mr. Keating and I are not friends. We're not even buddies, we're not chums, and we are not Christian brothers. We will treat each other civilly here today, because the issue is not Mr. Keating and Mr. Blackburn. The issue is truth. What is truth? You see, both of us cannot be right. One cannot be more right than the other. If one of us is right, the other one is totally wrong, and this is the whole issue that we're going to deal with. We are not separated brethren. Some of you don't know this, but years ago a Christian was not looked upon as a separated brethren, and a Catholic was not looked upon as a Christian. As Mr. Keating made reference last night, if you ask a Catholic, "Are you a Christian?" they'd say, "No, I'm a Catholic," because there was a great distinction between them. If we went back hundreds and hundreds of years, people who hold my position would be killed by the Catholic Church. They would never be looked upon as separated brethren. So, let's really see what the issue is today.

There are people here today, as the moderator said, who've got some prejudiced minds, and before this day is over, you'll probably be more prejudiced toward me. That's neither here nor there. The truth, when it comes forth, does one of two things. It either softens your heart or it hardens your heart. This debate is a result of some articles that were printed in the paper. And no one has come forth to refute the articles, which were referring to me, because I just gave the truth. I just gave history. I just gave the doctrines. No one came forth. I answered an invitation to come to a Bible study at a Catholic church, and I went to the Bible study. Not only did they not ask me back, but when I came the next week they were holding it somewhere else and didn't even let me know where it was at.

I don't want to get excited, but I want to tell you something. It is a reproach to any leadership that they have to hire somebody to defend their doctrines. You can come to my church, and I can open the book, and I can defend my doctrines. I can take my book, the Bible, and I can defend my doctrines. It is a reproach, and I do say a reproach, because I've been called an embarrassment to the Protestant clergy here in town. That a man [the local Catholic pastor] who leads a flock cannot teach a flock—he has to have somebody such as Mr. Keating come in and explain the doctrines to you people of the Catholic Church, so you will know what you believe. That's kind of a sad status of affairs.

Mr. Keating is very skilled in the art of words. There'll be many issues that he'll not touch upon or deal with, but he'll go off to the right or off to the left when asked a direct question. In his book *Catholicism and Fundamentalism* he touches very lightly on a major issue which to me is a focal point of the Catholic Church. In the horrible, horrendous murders that she committed throughout the Dark Ages on Christians and non-Christians alike who would not adhere to her doctrines or not adhere to the pope's supremacy.

For example, the St. Bartholomew's Day massacre in the 1600s. The only sin of the Huguenots was that they would not acknowledge the pope as the supreme authority. And so, on a Sunday when they were all in church, they were killed, massacred, the whole town was. Now, he touches lightly on this. I say lightly because of this fact. He focuses more on the erroneous data and the erroneous numbers that the historian gave. If you will take notice of how often Mr. Keating does this tactic, then you will get to see what this is all about today, what we are talking about.

How many of you here were at the seminar last night, the meeting? Great. I want to ask you a question. If I asked you to take your brains out, your mental capacity, and set it in your back pocket and sit down on it, and then open your mouth and let me shovel some stuff into you, how many of you would agree to that? Well, you know what you did last night? Exactly what I asked you to do now that you said you wouldn't do. Now, I will prove this today. I'm not making idle statements.

Last night the statement was made about the assumed vow of chastity that Mary made. Now, I want to ask you something because he made a big joke out of this. You know, like, when the Holy Spirit told Mary she was going to have a child, she says, "Well, I know that. Any Jewish girl who is going to get married is going to have a kid. That's no big thing." He said, so, she must have said, "How can this be that I know no man?" because she made a vow of chastity. Now, let me ask you something. I want you to raise your hand. I want you to be honest with me. How many of you would have married your mate if he or she had told you that they had taken a vow of chastity? One of you. Well, good. You're honest. I respect that.

Let me tell you something. Joseph wouldn't have married Mary if she'd taken a vow of chastity. But regardless, see he stopped right at verse 34 of Luke. If you will go to verse 35, you find the Holy Spirit explaining to Mary how this can be that she has not known a man and she is going to be pregnant. Because it wasn't time for her to be married yet, and she knew she couldn't commit any of those things without being put away and the Holy Spirit said, "It's simple Mary. The Holy Spirit is going to come upon you and you shall conceive." And he explained to her that she was going to get pregnant by the Holy Ghost. She didn't make a vow of chastity. Before this day is over, I'll take you through the Scriptures, show you the subterfuge that he used to disprove that she had children. And I'll show you that she did have children. I don't have to play with your mind, the Bible says it, and it says it so clearly, and so plainly—it's irrefutable.

Now, there are three types of people here today. Some of you are what we call unwittingly ignorant. You don't know that you don't know. Lots of us in this world are that way. All of us are that way about various subjects. There is a lot of things I don't know about. I'm unwittingly ignorant.

There are those who are knowingly ignorant. They know they don't know what they should know to do what they want to do, and they don't know how to go about it. This is especially true in the area of religion. Many of you people believe what you've been taught, hoping and praying that what you've been taught is true. And this man has come in to affirm to you that it is true, but he's the only assurance you have. If he is lying to you you're in a world of hurt. If I can prove to you that he has been lying to you, you have to make up your mind what's the truth here. Not, is Mr. Blackburn sharper than Mr. Keating? Did he do a better job of putting him down? That's not going to happen. I don't know enough about this man to discredit him, but I do know enough of what he's been doing to discredit the teaching.

Finally there is what we call the willingly ignorant. Those are people who say, "I don't care. I'm going to believe this way, nothing is going to change my mind. I was born a Baptist, I was born a Catholic, I was born a Mormon, I was born this or that, and I'm going to live that way, and I'm going to die that way." That's being willingly ignorant, in spite of the material that's brought before you, the facts that are brought before you, you've chosen to remain that way.

I want you to take a look at something. He said this last night, if you remember, that Mary's offering, when she came on the eighth day after Jesus was born for circumcision, was the offering to redeem the son. He used the Scripture in Leviticus to tell you that the first one has to be redeemed. Well, if you bothered to read your Bible, if you would look in Leviticus, you would find that in chapter 12:6–8, you were to bring a lamb but also you were to bring a sin offering and a burnt offering which was a pigeon or a turtle dove, because a woman who had a child was unclean. If you had no lamb, if you were from a poor family, you had to bring two pigeons or two turtle doves; one for a sin offering and one for a burnt offering. You will see, in Luke 1, that Mary and Joseph brought two turtle doves or two pigeons. Why? One was for her burnt offering because she was unclean after she had the baby, and the other was for a sin offering because they didn't have a lamb to redeem their baby. Now, that's in the Scriptures. Says it plain. I don't have to play with your mind and give you assumptions.

MODERATOR: Thank you, Rev. Blackburn. Now, we will have the fifteen minutes of opening remarks from Karl Keating.

KEATING: Last night, when I spoke at the base chapel [at Naval Air Weapons Station China Lake], I was able to give an explanation from the Bible of quite a few Catholic beliefs. I had the luxury of giving the positive side of the Catholic faith. Today, I'm on the defensive. The topic is, "What Is the Truth about the Catholic Church?" Mr. Blackburn has begun by saying there isn't much truth in it. He said a lot of other things, some of which I'll rebut at the appropriate time.

I was asked out to Ridgecrest some time ago. I was told that in this community there has been considerable anti-Catholic sentiment stated in the press, whether in letters or in ads, much of it crude, all of it wrong. Crude? Yes, such as the insult given to those of you who were at the seminar last night, the suggestion that you checked your brains at the door and that that's how the Catholic Church works. Apparently that also applies to the many Protestants who were there last night. So, if you're Protestant and you were there last night, you have to feel as insulted as the Catholics.

I've never found in the many seminars that we've given that anyone— Catholic, Protestant, Mormon, Jehovah's Witness, agnostic—checks his brain at the door. People come to find the truth, in love. They don't always agree, but that's why they're there.

Mr. Blackburn said, "There's a great reproach against the local Catholic Church, that it had to hire an outsider to come in and explain the Catholic religion." Let me make it clear. The Catholic Church doesn't pay for my organization. When we go around the country, we don't ask dioceses to fund us. We are not employees of the Church. This is precisely why we are a lay organization. If a priest were doing this, to the frequency that we are, people such as Mr. Blackburn would say, "Ah, you can't be telling the truth because you get a salary from the bishop." Couldn't the same complaint be made against a Protestant minister, getting a salary from his congregation? But I wouldn't bring up such a silly complaint.

"By their fruits you will know them." If you look around you'll find that there are no active anti-Episcopalians, no active anti-Methodists, no active anti-Quakers. No one takes out ads in the newspaper to run down these other religions. No one writes mean-spirited letters full of all kinds of exaggerations about these religions, but a lot of anger is vented at the Catholic Church, especially by ex-Catholics. It's much like the fellow who jilts his girlfriend and then, to make himself look good, bad-mouths her. We've all seen that happen. And here leaving the Mother Church, which is the Church that Jesus Christ founded, we find many people making it their profession or their avocation to spread false information about the Catholic faith. There is often little concern for the truth. What usually happens is that a partial truth is connected to a substantial fabrication. You can't get along in this country telling straight out lies. Nobody would believe that. But if you get something that's partly true, but misstate the facts, you can make headway.

I'll give you a couple of examples. Did you ever hear the story of the Catholic Church chaining the Bible so that Catholic lay people couldn't read it? It's true that the Church chained the Bible. Now, why did it do that? To keep it away from the people? No. To keep it *for* the people. Have you ever been in a telephone booth and found there a telephone directory? It's chained isn't it? Why? To keep it away from the people who want to use the telephone, or to keep it there for their use? Well, it's obvious. To keep it there for their use. In olden days, when Bibles were hand copied, a Bible would cost, in today's terms, as much as $10,000. It might be the only book in a town. It would be left on a table near the pulpit in the church for all to read but chained to that table so no one could steal it. As a matter of fact, after the Reformation in England, a country where Bibles had been chained, the Protestant Reformers ended up chaining many more than the Catholics ever had. As you see, when that charge is given by itself, it looks very black against the Catholic Church, but, when you look at the facts, you see it makes a lot of sense.

Let's go on to another topic, the Inquisition. The comment was made that millions of people, uncountable numbers of people, have been killed under the Inquisition and at other times by the Catholic Church. I deal with this question in my book. Reputable scholars will acknowledge that about three thousand people died during the centuries of the Inquisition. I'm not defending that, but that's the approximate number. Catholics and Protestants came up with that figure. I'm sure that Mr. Blackburn will not defend the fact that during early Reformation England, 800 people a year were burned at the stake for witchcraft. Of course, they weren't witches. In fact, there were many more people killed in England alone than during that entire Inquisition.

That the Protestant Reformers in England engaged in a punishment that we find horrible doesn't argue against the Protestant position. And the fact that six centuries ago some Catholics engaged in similar activities doesn't argue against the Catholic faith. All it argues for is that there are people on both sides throughout history who often lacked a sense of proportion and who sinned. Some of those people had positions of power, and they were able to exert their influence on others, even to the point of execution.

Swipes at Catholic history are a quiet acknowledgment that the Fundamentalist side has no history to talk about. Fundamentalism as a religious movement can be traced back only about a century. The name itself exists only since the time of World War I. It is not the same as Reformation Protestantism. Luther and Calvin and Zwingli would not agree with Mr. Blackburn, in his positions, and their positions are less than 500 years old. They're not the positions of the historical Christian Church. Whatever else you can say, if you say the Catholic Church cannot be the Church of Jesus Christ, you must admit that none of these upstart churches could be the one he established—unless, perhaps, you take the position of the Mormons, that his Church entirely disappeared and many centuries later popped-up with the advent of a new prophet, but I don't believe you take such a position.

It was suggested that, if one side is right, the other cannot be partially right. It must be totally wrong. That doesn't make sense. Consider, say, two political candidates, one with whom you agree entirely. Does that mean you disagree entirely with everything the other candidate professes? Very unlikely. Probably the two candidates agree on most things and differ on a few major or minor matters. Much the same when it comes to a question of truth. What I said last night, and what already has been misrepresented, is that only from the Catholic Church will you find the fullness of biblical Christianity, because it alone is the Church that Jesus Christ established. The Catholic Church always has acknowledged, not just since Vatican II, that other churches maintain truth in greater and lesser degrees.

For example, the Eastern Orthodox churches split off from the Catholic Church in 1054. The Eastern Orthodox believe the same things we do on almost every point. There are few points on which they disagree with Catholic teaching. The Catholic Church never claimed that everything those churches taught was incorrect. Not at all. That's not the Church's position. When it comes to Protestants, every Protestant church, in greater and lesser degrees, teaches truly, which is to say it teaches many things that are true but some things that are not. For example, almost every Protestant church teaches the

Trinity. When it does so, it teaches just the way the Catholic Church teaches. Some Protestant churches teach the imminent Second Coming of Christ, a theory that happens to be incorrect. To that extent, those churches teach something that is not true, but the fact that those churches teach some things that are not true doesn't mean that everything they teach is untrue.

I hope, as this afternoon continues, there's going to be a real effort to talk about truth and light, not falsehood and mere heat. Thank you.

MODERATOR: Thank you Mr. Keating. And now we will have a ten-minute rebuttal from Rev. Blackburn.

BLACKBURN: My telling the truth does not make me a bad person, folks. I didn't start this little charade, this little put-together. It was his group that put an article in the paper that said, "Jesus is not going to return," as he just said. That those of us who believe in the pre-millennial return of Christ are not teaching the truth. Well, listen, if Jesus isn't coming we have no hope. But that's what he said. And I just responded to that article, and I got called all kinds of names, and all I did was to respond to him. I have copies of every article in my scrap book if you'd like to see and find out the claims that I made. There is not a one that can't be backed up by historical fact.

Secondly, he talks about reputable scholars who will say there were only about three thousand killed. Listen, there were twenty or thirty thousand killed in one city. What do you mean three thousand killed in a span of time?

Now, let's go on a little further here. Fundamentalists can be traced back a hundred years. Can you imagine that? Folks, we can go back to Genesis 3 and find a Fundamentalist by the name of Abel who brought forth a bloody offering, and his brother tried to bring forth a bloodless offering, and God said, "I'll have nothing to do with that bloodless offering." We can trace Fundamentalism back from Noah to Abraham, from Abraham to Isaac, from Isaac to Jacob, to Israel, all the way up to Christ, and to the Church that Jesus Christ established that still carries on Fundamentalism and the truth of the Gospel.

The Catholic Church is not the Church Jesus founded. She came right in—you pick her history up—and became formalized around the year 300 or 325. You find the very thing that she did was start, again, to kill those who would not align with her. Why? Because she had the secular arm on her side, just like the Jews did. They had the Romans' secular arm on their side so they could arrest somebody and get the secular arm to kill him. It's just what happened throughout Catholic history. It's going to happen, again, one of these days when the secular arm and the religious arm unite again.

He made a statement last night, if you recall. He said that the beast in revelation was Nero. Did I misunderstand him, or did he say that? He said it was Nero, didn't he? Did you know that Nero reigned in 64 A.D.? Did you know that John, who wrote Revelation, wrote it after 64 A.D., and the Bible says there that he looked upon the beast and he was amazed. He couldn't believe that Christianity "had come to this cause." Why would John be amazed if he knew it was Nero who was already dead? Uh-uh, folks, something is wrong with that theology there.

Let me ask you something here. And I'm just going to read it to you because I know most of you don't have a Bible, or you don't have it with you, and I'm not trying to be sarcastic, but it tells us this. It says in John 1:13, if you want to take a note. It says, "which were born," speaking of men "born again." See, he says that we cannot find a born-again man before now. Let me tell you what. In 1 Peter 1:23 it says, "Who were born again, not by corruptible seed but by the word of God that liveth and abideth forever." I can take you back at least eighteen or nineteen hundred years and tell you there were born-again people there. And there still are. And they're getting them every day. And, praise God, if God opens any ears up here today, there'll be some more born again before this thing is over with.

I've been baptized, I've been confirmed, my kids were confirmed, I even took on the name when we went through confirmation. My son over there, who's with us, was confirmed. His name was John, my name is Jim. He took on the name of St. James, and I took on the name of St. John when we got confirmed. Listen, it didn't mean a thing. Neither one of us were Christians. We went through the rituals. There was a lady there last night that made a statement. She said, "I wish you could help me tell my Fundamentalist in-laws that the sprinkling baptism my baby has received is just as good as the dunking that they have in the Baptist church."

Let me tell you something: she's exactly right. The sprinkling baptism is just the same as the dunking baptism. There is no difference because neither one of them affects salvation. Neither one of them does a thing except get the baby wet. There is nothing in baptism that is sanctimonious [sic] and holy. Now, I know he is going to tell you the holy Church tells you differently, and I know she does, but there is nothing in the Scriptures that tell you that. If you would search out baptism in the Scriptures, you'd find the only ones that ever got baptized were those who believed. Folks, an eight-day-old baby cannot confess its sins and believe, and you can't confess them for him and make him believe.

If this gentleman is wrong about the teachings that he's teaching you, if they are anti-scriptural and he's teaching basically what the Catholic Church does teach—if he's wrong, you folks are in a lot of trouble, because you trusted the Church to be right. You'll not be able to stand before God one day and say, "My priest taught me, and I believed him, so it's his fault, not mine." Not when we have this book.

Before this day is over, I'm going to read you some things. You're not going to believe your ears, but it comes from the Catholic book. It comes from the Catholic Church: her beliefs, her teachings on the Word of God. You're going to have to make up your mind about it. I'm not going to do little verbal run-arounds with him. I'm concerned about presenting the truth. And if I can just get you one little truth that will make you stop and think, then I've done something. Now, I don't imply that you came in there and sat on your brains, but if you bought what he said last night, yes, you did.

MODERATOR: Thank you, Rev. Blackburn. Now we will have a ten minute rebuttal from Mr. Keating.

KEATING: So many errors, so little time.

Mr. Blackburn said the Bible says nothing about baptism doing anything to you. In my Bible, I find in the Epistle to Titus 3:5-7: "He saved us by the washing and regeneration in renewal in the Holy Spirit, so that we might be justified by his grace." What is the washing of regeneration? That's baptism. That's how Paul uses that phrase. The footnote to these verses in the Revised Standard Version, which is a Protestant translation, says that this is a brief and clear statement of the doctrine of justification. It explains that it is through baptism the soul becomes regenerated and the person becomes justified in God's sight.

Look at Acts 2:38: "Repent and be baptized every one of you in the name of Jesus Christ for the forgiveness of your sins, and you shall receive the gift of the Holy Spirit." Notice the sequence. First, repent. Then, baptism, which provides forgiveness. Then you get the Holy Spirit, which is to say God's grace. Baptism actually produces the forgiveness. That's what the Bible teaches. That's not what some Protestants teach, but they overlook certain passages of the Bible. They overlook history too. Did you catch the comment that the Catholic Church began in 325? That was it, just a bland phrase thrown out. No support. Why no support? Because there is no support. I give much of a chapter in my book to this type of Fundamentalist history. It's not enough just to make the claim.

What they say is that in 325 Christianity became legal, and then pagans rushed into the Church with their pagan ideas, corrupting it, and the Christian Church became the Catholic Church. If that were true, it would be only after 325 that we would see any alleged Christians professing distinctively Catholic beliefs, such as belief in priestly ordination, the Real Presence and the sacraments, confessing to a priest, a hierarchy in the Church, and the veneration of saints. We should expect those to come up only after 325 if this theory is true. But look at early Christian writings—I quote them at length in *Catholicism and Fundamentalism*. All these things, all these peculiarly Catholic beliefs, were believed in before 325. So the whole theory is out the window.

I know that Mr. Blackburn has my book. Perhaps he's not got to that chapter yet, but I hope he continues to read it because I explain there, for Protestants as well as Catholics, why that was the case. He said the Christianity of the New Testament really was Fundamentalism. Even Adam was a Fundamentalist, even Paul was a Fundamentalist. This is nonsense, ladies and gentlemen. Fundamentalism as a religious term denotes a particular set of beliefs that were not held, as a set, by any Christians until the last century or so.

I acknowledge that Fundamentalists have mostly truths in their religion, but they also have beliefs that are inventions of recent years. And you can't get those new beliefs from the New Testament. I notice one thing always happens. It's claimed this or that New Testament passage means the same as what Fundamentalists today teach. The connection is never drawn very well. Nothing is said of the intervening 1,900 years. Why? Because you will not find evidence, especially in the first 1,500 years, of anybody believing those things. If they were believed by the New Testament authors, we should expect them to be written about by writers in the first, second, and third centuries, but we don't find that.

Mr. Blackburn suggested that last evening I said that Jesus would not return. No, I didn't say that. Maybe he didn't tune in a few days ago when I had a radio debate with Dave Hunt, who is one of the most popular dispensational pre-millennialists in the country. Dave and I talked about this very question. The Catholic position and the majority of traditional Protestant positions since the Reformation—the position, really, of all Protestants until the last few decades—has been that Jesus would return at the end of time but that his return is not imminent. We find that people who are influenced by this dispensational school have a tendency to see the Second Coming right around the corner, and they always are trying to put America in a key place in the Book of Revelation.

Of course, America is not mentioned in Scripture. Years ago Hal Lindsey in his *Late Great Planet Earth* predicted that 1975 would be the time and that didn't happen. Then 1981 was to be the rapture and the tribulation. That didn't happen. Our Lord said we're not going to know the day or the hour. He did say he would return. The Catholic Church has always taught this, but we don't know when that will be. There is no teaching in the Bible about seven so-called dispensations. That was an invention, in the nineteenth century, by John Nelson Darby of the Plymouth Brethren denomination. His theory was unknown by Christians before his time, Catholic and Protestant. He simply made it up.

What about Mary's sin offering? Did she make the sin offering? Yes, she did. Does that mean that she committed sins? No. Perhaps Mr. Blackburn forgot what Jesus did when he commanded Peter to throw the line in the water and bring out a fish. In the mouth of that fish was a coin. "Render to Caesar," he said, "what is Caesar's, to God what is God's." Remember something else Jesus said. He did this not because he was under any obligation to do so, but he did it to conform with the law, to do all that was in the law so as not to give scandal to others. Mary, of course would do the same, because the townsfolk didn't know our Lord's status. Mary and Joseph didn't go about and say, "This is the Son of God. The conception was miraculous, the birth miraculous." No. The people thought the child was Joseph's own. Jesus and his parents were concerned to fulfill the law in all ways so as not to give scandal to anyone. And they did that. Jesus perfected the law, but he never violated the law.

Joseph wouldn't have married Mary, we're told, if he had known about her vow. The Bible doesn't say that anywhere. The Bible doesn't hint that anywhere. This is just a conclusion drawn out of thin air. If you can swallow the fact that God takes human flesh, which is the biggest miracle of all, you can swallow the very minor inconveniences that the Holy Family might have had inasmuch as it was not the average family on the block. It was not like yours or mine, with average kids. Its one child was a special child.

I'm saying that, yes, God would have provided specially for Mary. I explained last night that Mary had to be married, else, at the birth of Jesus, she would have been stoned to death because the crowds would have thought she had committed fornication or adultery. She had to be married. Is it beyond possibility that someone such as St. Joseph could have so much love for God and for Mary that he would enter into such a marriage, rather than a normal marriage? Is it possible a man could do that? I think St. Joseph, under God's grace, could do such a thing and did do such a thing.

MODERATOR: This next segment, we're going to have a cross-examination. We will begin by Rev. Blackburn asking Mr. Keating a question. He will have

30 seconds to ask the question. Mr. Keating will have two minutes to respond to the question, and then we will allow one minute rebuttal on the part of Rev. Blackburn. Then we will alternate.

BLACKBURN: I'll ask Mr. Keating, because I want this defined for my understanding. In his book—and by the way, I have read all of his book. I've got footnotes all over it. In fact, I have to buy his book from the guy who gave it to me because I've got so many footnotes in it, I can't give it back to him. I scratched his book all up, writing in it. So, if you see me purchase one, I'm not buying it because I'm interested in it, but I owe it to the guy who gave it to me.

Could you please define, because you make the statement on page 275, paragraph 3, that although the Scripture is completely silent on the Assumption of Mary, because the Church teaches it as being true, we are guaranteed that it is true? Now, I want to know what that church is that you are talking about, that guarantees it. Please don't say it's the Catholic Church. I need the definition of that church that makes these decisions, makes these theological interpretations out of where there is nothing.

KEATING: In my book, I'm referring to the Catholic Church when I use the shorthand "the Church" with a capital C. Reading my book, that's clear. This Church is precisely the Church that Jesus Christ founded. It is his body extended throughout time and history. It is that vine of which he spoke, that kingdom of which he spoke. Does it have an institutional aspect? Yes, it does. It has a human aspect, because we are members of this Church. But Jesus Christ is the ultimate head of this Church because he founded it. He granted to it his own authority and his own power, and included in that power was the power to teach truly. The Christian Church had to have that power. The one thing it had to have is infallibility because souls and their destiny were at stake, were the Church to teach in error. He gave that power to the Church because he himself had it. That power allows the Church to explain and to work out the doctrines given by Jesus to the apostles, passed on to them through Sacred Tradition down to our own time.

There may be something, such as the Assumption, which is not explicitly mentioned in Scripture, certainly not by name. Of course, the Trinity is not mentioned by name either. Does this argue against its actuality? The Bible does not claim to be a catechism or theological treatise. It wasn't even written for non-Christians. Every book of the New Testament was written for people already Christian. Much of the latter part, the epistles, were written to Christians who were having problems, confusions. The New Testament, in no place, claims to be a complete delineation of all Christian teaching.

MODERATOR: Brother Blackburn, you have one minute.

BLACKBURN: I didn't get my answer. I got the same thing I got last night. Am I right or wrong?

VOICE: You're wrong.

BLACKBURN: Okay. Then you tell me what the church is folks, because he sure didn't tell me. He just said it's the Catholic Church. What is that entity that makes the decisions that you believe? That's all I'm trying to find out. I see a segregated aspect. The pope, the priests, the bishops, the intellectuals, the theologians tell you how you can become a member of the Church. The Bible says that we are members in the body of Christ. I see that the church that Christ puts forth is led by the Holy Spirit. But we, evidently, don't have it because we have to look to them for leading, and that's anti-scriptural. The Bible tells us that the anointing that we have will teach us and that we need no man to teach us.

KEATING: My question to Mr. Blackburn is this: if Mary did have children, other than our Lord, why was there no mention of her having other children in any writing outside of and after the New Testament, by any person claiming to be a Christian, whether heretic or Catholic? Why was there no claim at all until the year 380 when Helvetius made the claim?

BLACKBURN: This is an easy one, folks. The people who conquer usually write history, so what history we have, we have the Catholic Church's because they conquered the Christians, so they burned all the books and the Bibles and the history. You've not studied what I have. Let me tell you something. Look at John 19:25, which he used last night, about the three Marys at the Cross. It explicitly gives those three Marys: Mary Magdalene, Mary the wife of Cleophas, and Mary the Mother of Jesus. You find those three Marys at the Cross with their sons James and Joseph.

Now Mr. Keating used the son James to show you the ambiguity of it that James could be the son of this or that. Why didn't he use Joseph? I'll tell you why, because every place you find Joseph in the New Testament outside the Joseph of Arimathea, Joseph the Levite, and the husband of Mary, you find this one particular Joseph with Mary the Mother of Jesus. Identification. It just seemed so natural, since her husband was named Joseph that her son would be named Joseph. She had no choice in Jesus. The angel said he is already named. But you find this Joseph in Matthew 13:53. Everywhere you find Mary, the mother of Jesus, you find her son Joseph.

KEATING: Please note that, by default, he proved my case. He did not name any writer between the time of the New Testament and the year 380 who claimed at all that Mary had children other than Jesus. There are none. He claims that all the writings were destroyed. We have lots of writings from heretics in those centuries. Lots of writings that are in libraries. They weren't destroyed. We have writings which are against every other Catholic doctrine. Why not this? The claim is that the Catholic Church destroyed the Bible. I would like to point out to Mr. Blackburn that, were it not for the Catholic Church preserving the Bible, you wouldn't have one at all.

BLACKBURN: You got that backwards. Let's not get into a shouting match. I'm about to shout myself already.

MODERATOR: Ladies and gentlemen I would like to caution you, please, to keep your comments to yourself. I know how difficult that can be, but the amens, hallelujahs, hooray brother, whatever, please keep them, because once it starts and we open the door, we could end up having a real rhubarb. That's not what we're here for. We're here to let these gentlemen explain their positions. So, I will ask you, again, please withhold any comments. Thank you. Rev. Blackburn.

BLACKBURN: I would ask Mr. Keating to explain again as he did last night, because I didn't get it clearly, when he talked about praying in vain repetitions, if he would please clarify that for me.

KEATING: My remark last night was that the reference can't be used against the rosary because the essence of what Jesus was saying happened to deal with the word "vain." I explained at some length why the prayers of the pagans, the heathens, were vain because they were praying to gods who did not exist. That's why they were vain. Jesus did not condemn repetition in prayer. In fact, he repeated prayers himself in the Garden of Gethsemane. I said, if you are to say that he condemns repeated prayer, you must conclude that he is a hypocrite, which just cannot be the case. The other thing I would point out is the claim that the prayers in the rosary are prayers you ought not to say, yet the Hail Mary is a prayer composed from clauses taken out of Scripture. The Our Father, of course, was given to us by our Lord. There is nothing in the rosary at all opposed to the Bible.

BLACKBURN: Last night he gave us a little clear example when he started talking about how they would name Jupiter and call him all kinds of names, all the names named for the gods. And they would go through all these names, and names, and names, until they finally got through all the names and then they would make the request right quick. You termed that vain repetitions. I'd like to read you something from the 1959 Catholic missal. It's called a litany. I think there must be forty different names that they put here to Jesus. And then they finally say, "Be merciful, and save us from all sins," and so forth. That's the same situation, folks. It's vain, repetitious prayers. And it's not just a prayer, it's a programmed prayer. Not something from your heart, just say this over and over and all these blessings come from it. That's vain repetition.

MODERATOR: Next question.

KEATING: Let me glide into a question that is similar to a previous one. Perhaps I can get a more direct answer. If Jesus is not present, really, in the Holy Eucharist, why was there no written opposition to this by any Christian, or alleged Christian, until the eleventh century, with Berengarius of Tours? If the Real Presence was an invention, why did no Christian write against it until that point?

BLACKBURN: We have your statement that no Christian wrote against it, but we don't know that for a fact. Just as there is much history we don't know. But I think because it was so silly nobody considered that anybody could possibly believe something like that. Look in John 4 and you'll find that Jesus is talking to the woman at the well, and the disciples come to him and ask him about getting something to eat. He said, "I have meat that you know not of and my food is to do my Father's will." Now if you want to tell me that when Jesus worked, he got physically nourished, then I'll accept that when Jesus passed the bread out, that they really ate his body.

KEATING: I think the honest person has to say there is something wrong with a religious position that works by conspiracy theory, that says, "Oh, I can't find any opposition to your point in history, or any support for mine, because it must have all been destroyed." That's somewhat like those people who go around nowadays saying, "Oh, the Holocaust never happened under the Nazis" and that all the evidence was faked. Or "Neil Armstrong never made it to the Moon, and it was all done in a studio in Hollywood." There are people who think that, but I don't think they're credible, and there are people who think that, conveniently, all the tough things disappeared in history. I don't buy that either.

MODERATOR: Your question, sir.

BLACKBURN: Would you please explain to me what an indulgence is?

KEATING: An indulgence is a grant of God's own merciful benefaction to a soul in purgatory by which that soul is cleansed more quickly of that self-love that still remains in it and that prevents it from going into heaven and enjoying the Beatific Vision. An indulgence, some people say, was a thing which prompted the Protestant Reformation. In fact it was not. True, Luther did have some complaints about indulgences in his Ninety-Five Theses, but that wasn't the cause of the Reformation. The ultimate cause for Luther and for Calvin was the question "Where does authority lie?" Not the question of indulgences.

At the time of Luther were there people who were misrepresenting what indulgences were? Yes, there were, and popes came out and condemned them. But remember in those days there were no telephones or telegraphs. Communication was slow and the papacy, really, quite weak. It was not always able to straighten out people who were going off onto their own tangents, such as Friar Tetzel in Germany. Luther had a legitimate annoyance, but I'm afraid in his case he threw out the baby with the bath water. Indulgence is a historical and true Christian doctrine. It's an example of God's great mercy to sinners.

BLACKBURN: Never did get a clarification of what an indulgence is, but I understand it, from my experience, was that if you sin you could build up things that would take care of some of your sins. So if you had 45 indulgences, they might be good for one venial sin or two venial sins. I don't know the amount, but in essence, you could buy off your sins with your good works. Now I don't know if that's what he's trying to say, but he's saying that something happens in purgatory, that if you have indulgences you evidently don't suffer as long. So they must be buying them off. And I don't find any place in Scripture where it says you can do things to build up against the sins you're going to commit.

KEATING: Scripture doesn't say and the Catholic Church has never taught you could do things to get a reservoir of brownie points so that you could have certain sins you don't have to worry about.

MODERATOR: This is your question period.

KEATING: Sorry. This is my rebuttal, is it not?

MODERATOR: No, this is your question.

KEATING: Then I will switch my question. My question is this: the Bible nowhere lists its own contents. It doesn't list the books that make it up. How does the Bible Christian know what books belong in the Bible and what books don't belong in the Bible?

BLACKBURN: Primarily, we know that the books of the Bible were canonized and, I'm not even going to get into the silly argument, the Catholic Church, they're the ones that did it, so they're responsible for the Bible. We know that's not true. God is. But, we can tell through the harmony of the Scriptures. There is not a passage from Scripture or a document in the Bible, or a book in the Bible that you can't find the harmony. This is one of the criteria when they made up and canonized those books that they wanted to be in the Scriptures: did they harmonize with the rest of the Scripture? This is the reason, and I'm sure Mr. Keating knows, but will not admit it, that the Apocrypha part of the Catholic Bible is not accepted by Bible scholars because it doesn't harmonize with the rest of the Scriptures. It actually conflicts with it. But, the books are made up by study of the Scriptures, affirming that they are God's word by the authors who were the apostles, and the harmony of it. We know that there was a book or a letter written by Paul to the Corinthians. There was a third letter to the Corinthians, but for what reason God chose not to have it stay in existence or have it put into the Scriptures, I don't know. God did that. You see, God has said that he will preserve the Scriptures, his word.

Now, I note Mr. Keating uses that to say that's the Church. But the issue there is in Isaiah 51:19, I believe: "The word that I put in your mouth and my spirit will not depart forever from your children's mouth," and so forth and so on. God preserved his word. And if you would look through the Scriptures under preservation, you would discover God has done exactly that because he's promised it over and over. It's not in mankind's ability to preserve God's word. We're so full of errors and mistakes. So you have to look at the harmony of it and then you'll know which books are which. It's easy to do, if you want to study. But I know it's a scholarly job and most laymen don't do that. I tell you this much, don't even believe what I'm saying today without studying it out for yourself. I ask none of you to believe me on my word.

KEATING: The problem with the harmony theory is that it simply won't work. Take, for example, the Didache, the teaching of the twelve apostles, written about the year 70. Nothing in it is objectionable to Protestants. Yet it was not put in as an inspired book of the Bible. It harmonizes perfectly. Take, for example, the book of Philemon, the epistle to Philemon. Read it for yourself. You'll find almost no doctoral content in it. Why would somebody put that in—because it harmonizes, because it simply doesn't contradict? In that case, you would have put in all sorts of other books. No, there had to be some judge to make the decision which books belong in the Bible. That was the Church that Christ established.

MODERATOR: Your question, Rev. Blackburn.

BLACKBURN: In your book you use the theologian Tertullian five times. Four of those times you use him as an authoritative reference to the sign of the cross, doctrinal issues or the development of doctoral issues, the papacy, and so forth and so on. But on the fifth issue, it comes to him refuting the perpetual virginity of Mary, and you dismiss him as a heretic. How can that be, that he can support you on one end but he can't on the other?

KEATING: When I refer to Tertullian—for example, mentioning the sign of the cross—I did it to show that there were Christian writers saying that that was already an old custom, to show that you can't very well go about saying, "Oh, this was invented in the Middle Ages." Tertullian did not write everything accurately. Others did not write everything accurately. My point in quoting Tertullian and many other early writers is just to show these things were believed by somebody at that time, as disproof of the notion that they were invented many centuries later. It's a very simple thing. Look in the book. Look at the references to him and to others. That's all I was doing, to show that the notion that the Church started after 325 just falls apart.

MODERATOR: One-minute rebuttal.

BLACKBURN: I can only say this: if I cannot accept the man's testimony because his credentials are bad, I cannot use him as a witness.

KEATING: Let's go back, if we may, to the question of repetitious prayer. Mr. Blackburn, you said we ought to avoid prayers, such as litanies which are praises of Jesus, because they are programmed. They are set prayers, which they are. Are we also, therefore to avoid the Our Father, which is a programmed set prayer?

BLACKBURN: There are so many doctoral issues set forth in the Our Father that you could say it, just one aspect of it, and pray on that for a long time. The disciples said, "Teach us how to pray." They knew how to pray. They're not asking for the instructional manual. They're talking about how do we revere God in our prayers. He said, "well you start off with 'hallowed be thy name,'" because if the name isn't hallowed, then you can't come into God. And it goes on, "We're pleased that your kingdom come, and that it be done here on Earth as it is in heaven." And it's a plea, again, for God to come and reign and rule. It's not a vain repetitious prayer, and that isn't our Lord's Prayer, by the way. Our Lord's Prayer you'll find in John 17. This is just a prayer that Jesus instructed them on how to pray. The Lord's Prayer is in John 17. It's not vain, repetitious.

KEATING: Just as we can meditate on the words within the Lord's prayer, we can meditate on any set prayer and its phrases in praise of God. And that's what we ought to do. I guess Mr. Blackburn agrees with me that there are programmed, set prayers that are good. That's a wonderful admission on his part.

MODERATOR: Question, Mr. Blackburn.

BLACKBURN: You tell me that the pope cannot make an infallible statement, *ex cathedra*, infallibly in the Church, because the Holy Spirit prevents him from doing such. But in 352 you had Pope Liberius, and when he was deposed, Felix took his place, and both of these adhered to and swore to the doctrine of the Arians, who taught that Christ was created and was lower than the Father.

KEATING: You got the facts wrong. The document that Liberius signed was written by Semi-Arians. That's different from Arianism. The Semi-Arians had an ambiguous phrase, not a heretical phrase. Liberius did it under coercion, political coercion. He was arrested and would not be released until he signed it, and the Catholic Church has always taught the pope does not teach infallibly unless he teaches freely. If he is tortured into signing something, it doesn't count. That's the same rule we have in courts of law in this country. Even if it had been a free signing, he was not teaching publicly something for all Christians to hold. Liberius, as I mentioned in my book, is one of only three potential cases to argue against papal infallibility. As I explain, they all collapse.

If popes have been teaching fallibly for all these centuries, you would think that they would come up with exactly contrary positions. Some pope would teach, for example, that the Resurrection never happened. That's what you need to show to disprove papal infallibility, but you can't show anything like that. You'd expect it out of normal human beings not under the protection of the Holy Spirit, but in fact the popes, in their official teachings, have never contradicted one another.

BLACKBURN: The Bible tells us in Isaiah that we are to compare Scripture with Scripture, line upon line, precept upon precept when we study the Scripture. It is not for us just to grab something up. You can reason things together. You can point them out. You can't take things out of context. This gentleman took the Church of Christ's position on baptismal regeneration in Acts 2:38: "Be baptized and repent for the remission of sin." There is a counter verse to that, in Luke, where two men are healed from leprosy, and they start going back and Jesus says, he says, "Go to the priest and make an offering for your healing." Now, if we take the word "for" in that context, then it means go make an offering so you can be healed, but he was already healed. The context of the Scriptures is go make an offering to the priest because of your healing. It's the same thing in Acts. You repent because of your sins, and you get baptized because you repented. Baptism never washes away. Look at Ephesians 5:25-26. It says, "He gave himself for the Church and he cleansed it by the washing of the water of the Word." You get it from studying the Scriptures, comparing Scripture with Scripture, not coming with these things, "Well, the Scripture doesn't talk about this."

KEATING: Even if you say we must compare one passage with another—which, of course, you should do—you're still are left with making an interpretation. No book can interpret itself. Interpretation is handled only by a person, an agent. You must do it with your mind and your heart. The Fundamentalist interprets the Bible on his own, and within Fundamentalism we find people at odds with one another. Post-millennialist against pre-millennialists and post-tribulationists—all these kinds of things. They're all born-again Fundamentalists. They disagree because they tried to do it on their own without a guide.

MODERATOR: Next question. We'll have time for two more. One from each of you.

BLACKBURN: Sir, you made a statement last night that it was okay to make statues, graven images. The Bible specifically says that you are not to make unto yourself a graven image. So would you reconcile how you can make a graven image when the Bible forbids it?

KEATING: What is a graven image? An image of some created thing worked by human hands. That's all it is. I mentioned that God told the Israelites in Exodus 25 to make images to adorn the Ark. He told them to make statues. It was commanded by God and therefore approved by God. I take God's word for it.

MODERATOR: Rebuttal.

BLACKBURN: I wish you really would. Now, God said to make the image, and if you'll look in Hebrews 8:5, you'll find that the Temple was a shadow of things in heaven, and no one got to go in and worship the images, or bow to those images, or do anything to them because the high priest went into the Holy of Holies. Nobody else could go in. They were an example or a type of the mercy seat where Jesus, when he ascended to heaven, sprinkled his blood on the mercy seat. But we are not allowed to make images or bow down before them. Now, I spent 17 years in the Catholic Church, and I've walked down the aisle and seen Jesus hanging on the cross, with the statue of the Virgin Mary, and bent down to do my genuflection, folks. The Bible says, no. Now, if he's going to take the Bible's word on it, he ought to practice what he preaches.

MODERATOR: Final question, Mr. Keating.

KEATING: I'd like to know why anti-Catholic Fundamentalists are so reluctant to look at and to appeal to early Christian history and writings? Why do they shy away from them and never use those writings to bolster their own position?

BLACKBURN: If you have a pencil and paper, write down these verses: Deuteronomy 4:2, Proverbs 30:5-6, Revelation 22:18-19, and Matthew 4:4.

The Bible says, "Add not to the word, take not away from the word." It says it three times, and then it adds this: when the Devil was testing Jesus, Jesus said, "Man shall not live by bread alone but by"—and I'll paraphrase Mr. Keating here—"some of the words in the Bible." No, the Scripture says, "Every word that proceedeth forth from the mouth of God." If it's not in the Scriptures, it's not legit. If you have to pervert the Scriptures to make it fit, it's not legit. I don't need anybody's Christian writings. I have the testimony and the word of God himself. Why do I need some man to tell me, "Well, he did this and he did that," even though it's contradictory to the word of God? I don't need that, nor will I practice it.

MODERATOR: One-minute rebuttal.

KEATING: I notice that you were free in making allusions to later Christian history and writings. Are those adding to the word of God? No. No Catholic claims that the early Christians, in the first, second, third centuries, wrote things that are being added to the word of God, when we merely appeal to them for evidence of what the early Christians believed. What did the first Christians understand the Gospel to be all about and to teach? That's a good way to find out the proper interpretation. But if we close our minds to that, put blinders over our eyes, we are cheating ourselves, and we are liable to come up with the wrong conclusions. That happens a lot with Fundamentalism.

MODERATOR: We're going to have now a 30-minute question-and-answer period. The first question will be to Rev. Blackburn. Then we will alternate. Rev. Blackburn will have two minutes to give an answer. Then Mr. Keating will have a one minute rebuttal period. We will continue like this for 30 minutes.

QUESTIONER: Rev. Blackburn, you stated that there is no problem with an individual interpreting Scripture on his own. I ask you this then: as of 1500, there was one Church, the Catholic Church. Since then the Bible's been turned loose into everyone's hands. Now, we've got over three thousand

Christian churches, all stating to be the one and only Church. I'll say three thousand even. That means two thousand nine hundred and ninety-nine say you're wrong. Seems to me that your theory has some fallacy to it.

BLACKBURN: Now, there can be three thousand, there can be ten thousand churches that say they are following Christ, and that's very possible. You see that Paul wrote to the churches in Galatia, he wrote to the churches at Corinth, the churches in Macedonia. He went to a number of churches. They are individual, local bodies, they're all autonomous. Nobody has a rule over anybody. If you want to check this out, look in Acts 15, where they have the big convention about what should we do, because some of the people were teaching that you had to be circumcised and keep the Law in order to be saved. The apostles got together and the rule went out, that they should abstain from meat, from blood, and from fornication. No other things. The churches are free to rule their own. There is no hierarchy, there's no ruling political body that tells you what to do. They can follow after Christ.

They are not the church of Christ per se, in that they are the only entity, such as the Catholic Church puts herself. But they're all churches that are following the Scriptures. They're not all known as Baptists, as Mr. Keating has referred to. Some were called the Anabaptist, some were called the Albigensians, some were the Donatists, some were the Montanists, some were the Waldensians, some were Huguenots, some were Paulicians, but it was the doctrines that they followed, and contrary to his word, you can trace them all the way back to Christ's time from today. You cannot trace the doctrines that are being taught today erroneously back to the apostles. The apostles never baptized babies. The apostles never taught baptismal regeneration. The apostles—

QUESTIONER: You didn't answer my question.

BLACKBURN: Okay. I'm sorry. I did not. The question was the amount of churches. There can be three thousand, there can be ten thousand churches that are following Christ.

MODERATOR: Karl Keating has a one minute rebuttal.

KEATING: The word church is used in two different senses in the New Testament. In Matthew 16:18 our Lord says, "Thou art Peter, and upon this rock I will build my Church," singular. He founded one Church. But Paul writes to many churches. What does that mean? Did Jesus found more churches? No. The Church, itself, is manifested in local communities of Christians. That's all it means. Today we use the term "church" for the actual building. It could be used in many senses. The fact is that these heretical groups that Mr. Blackburn listed did not all teach the same. The Albigensians believed in ritual suicide and that fornication was permissible, not immoral, and that marriage and the body are evil. You can't trace those teachings back to Jesus.

MODERATOR: Question for Mr. Keating.

QUESTIONER: Should Protestants and Catholics living today strive to keep all of the Ten Commandments including the Saturday Sabbath?

KEATING: Catholics and Protestants, of course, should do their utmost to maintain God's commandments, but it is not a doctoral matter what day of the week we worship God. In the book of Acts we find that the first Christians are meeting on what we call Sunday, when the Jews were meeting on what we call Saturday, the Sabbath, the last day of the week. This is purely a disciplinary thing. The early Church changed it. There was no complaint about it until many centuries later, at the time of the Reformation, when some Sabbatarian sects came up, and now we see, for example, the Seventh-day Adventists who say, "No, you have to go back to Saturday because that's what the Bible teaches." Well, that's strange because we had more than a millennium of Christians who did not teach that at all. As I said, it is merely a disciplinary decision as to what day of the week one is to worship God corporately, socially, in union. It could have been any, but the early Christians chose Sunday to be that day.

BLACKBURN: In the New Testament, all of the commandments are reiterated except the one to keep the Sabbath holy. If we study the Scriptures, we find that Jesus is our rest. In him we find rest, the Sabbath. He told the religious leaders that I am the Lord of the Sabbath and the Sabbath was made for man, man wasn't made for the Sabbath. Worship, mostly, is on Sunday. If people want to worship on Saturday, fine, as long as it doesn't become an issue of salvation, and some people make it an issue of salvation, that if you don't keep that commandment you can't be saved. That's not scriptural.

MODERATOR: Question for Rev. Blackburn.

QUESTIONER: Rev. Blackburn, you said that you were a Catholic for 17 years and this was not a childhood Catholicism. Would you please tell us the age at which you became a Catholic, the year that this happened and where it happened and what caused you to leave?

BLACKBURN: I became a Catholic in 1959 when I married my wife, who was born in a Catholic home, raised in a Catholic home, and attended Catholic schools, and so I converted to her religion. I had been raised as a Baptist. And I'll tell you why I converted to her religion, because a priest told me that as long as you don't over-indulge you don't sin. I liked to drink and I liked to party, and I liked to do all those things, and he told me that you can do anything you want to do as long as you don't do it to excess. So I converted to Catholicism. In 1977, we had a tragedy in our home that the Church could not meet. It could not heal, could not help. I found Jesus Christ, and so did my wife, and he healed, and he helped. From that day forth I started examining. It didn't matter to me what I believed because I had the Church taking care of me. She sheltered me, she took care of me and made sure that she was going to get me out of purgatory if I was bad. She was going to do all these things for me, and then I got to studying and discovered she couldn't do a thing for me, but Jesus could. That's the reason that I abide him today.

KEATING: Naturally, I can't rebut an individual's conversion story. I just want to refer, if I may, to one point he brought up about what the priest had said. To the extent I understand it, the priest was correct. Such things as drinking alcohol or smoking or gambling are not, in and of themselves, sins unless taken to extremes. Our Lord himself drank. He was accused of being a drunkard. He made water into wine after the guests had finished off the usual quantity of wine. Everybody had had some. He made more wine for the wedding. He was accused of being a drunkard because he was seen drinking wine. The Bible teaches is that these are good things if used properly, but anything can be misused.

QUESTIONER: I think you were right when you said that the main issue in the Reformation was authority, not necessarily grievances and indulgences and things like that. And I think the main issue of this debate is: are Catholics really going to heaven? Are Baptists really going to heaven? That's the issue, right? We all want to go to heaven. We don't want to go to hell. The question is, in Acts 2:38, you said repentance preceded the baptism. How does a two-week-old baby repent? If baptism is necessary to save you after repentance, then Catholics haven't been saved if they haven't been properly dunked.

KEATING: God does not require of us what is beyond our natural capacity. He does not require positive affirmation by a young child below the age of reason, what the Fundamentalists would commonly call "the acceptance of Christ as Lord and Savior." A young child cannot make such an affirmation, just as he cannot sin because he cannot use reason yet. Since the child is not able to do those kinds of things, the requirement is not held up to him. Jesus said, "Let the children come to me," and in John 3:5, he said, "You must be baptized. You must be born again of water and the Holy Spirit." That's baptism, and it applies to children. As I explained at some length last night, infant baptism is perfectly permissible and was practiced by the earliest Christians. There is no recorded complaint about it, and it in no way contradicts the Bible.

BLACKBURN: Again, studying the Scripture with Scripture, precept upon precept, you find that being born of water and the spirit refers back to Ephesians 5 where he washed him through the washing—he made him clean through the washing of the word. Born again by the infallible word. If baptism really regenerated people, we would wonder why John baptized all those people. In Acts 19 Paul came upon a bunch of people and all they had known was the baptism of John, and they weren't Christians. Paul preached the gospel to them, and they got saved, and it tells us that they received the Holy Spirit. If baptism had regenerated, Paul wouldn't have had to do that.

QUESTIONER: You mentioned a while ago that if we sin, we can confess it to the priest. In 1 Timothy 2:5 it says, "For there is one God and one mediator between God and man, the man Christ Jesus." And he also said, in 1 John 1:9, "If you confess your sins, he is faithful and just to forgive us our sins and to cleanse us from all unrighteousness." And also, in Matthew 11:28, he said that.

KEATING: He also said in John 20:22-23, to the apostles, "Whose sins you shall forgive, they are forgiven, whose sins you shall retain, they are retained." He gave his own authority to the apostles. He delegated his authority as principal to agent. That's in the Bible. There is no contradiction there. The priest does not forgive sins out of his own human power. He forgives sins only because Jesus has granted him the power. He could not do so otherwise. If you say no to that, you reject what Jesus says in John 20:22-23. There is no way around that.

BLACKBURN: That's a tough piece of Scripture. I realize that. But when we look at the history of it and we look at the facts of the Scripture in that this man that was supposed to be the rock, Jesus called Satan and told get behind me, God never entrusted in man the power to forgive sins. He never has. In John 9 you'll find that it is stated emphatically that only God can forgive sins.

QUESTIONER: Question for Mr. Blackburn. You stated that the Blessed Mother, Virgin Mary, whatever you care to refer to her as, is nothing more than an ordinary woman. Luke 1 states that Elizabeth, filled with the Holy Spirit, said, "Blessed art thou among women and blessed is the fruit of thy womb, Jesus." In that same chapter, it says, "All generations shall call me blessed," referring to the Blessed Mother. Could you state how you could possibly say that she's just an ordinary woman?

BLACKBURN: In the book of Judges we have a story of a gal by the name of Deborah who went to war. Deborah was called "blessed are you above all women." Not "blessed among, but blessed above all." Now we need to clarify something here in that Mary was blessed among women because she was chosen of God to bring his Son into this world. That would be a blessing any woman would love to have bestowed upon her, but she wasn't blessed because she was somebody. God could have used any virgin, and the only reason he used a virgin was because he prophesied that his Son would be born of a virgin. Had he prophesied his Son would be born of a 68-year-old grandma, he would have been born of a 68-year-old grandma, and they would have said of her, "Blessed are you among women, because you have given birth to the Savior." No merit on Mary's part whatsoever.

KEATING: When we look at the Greek, we see that the word used to describe Mary implies plentitude or fullness of grace, not just that she was a lucky gal because she got to give birth to the Savior. This is a quality inhering in herself, a condition of her own being—full of grace to the fullest extent possible for a creature. That's what the Greek implies, and that's what Christianity has understood consistently. Appeal, for example, to the Eastern Orthodox churches. They broke off, as I said, in 1054, but they teach this exactly.

QUESTIONER: Sir, please correct me if I heard you wrong, but I heard you say that there was an authority about the graven images from God. But in Exodus 20:4-5, it reads, "Thou shalt not make unto thee any graven image, or any likeness of anything that is in heaven above or that is in the earth beneath or that is in the water under the earth." And verse 5, "Thou shalt not bow down, exalt them nor serve them, for I, the Lord thy God, I am a jealous

God." Which is correct—what you have told us, that there was an authority from the Lord about graven images, or what we just read?

KEATING: You're putting the wrong spin on Exodus 20:4. Look at Exodus 25:18. That's where God told the Israelites to put statues on top of the Ark of the Covenant. He said, "Make them." The Ark, of course, was the object in which the Ten Commandments were kept. In the Temple that the Jews had in Jerusalem the priests would prostrate themselves in the Holy of Holies, bowing down before things created by men. In your wallet you probably have pictures of your family. Those are graven images. I don't think you would make Exodus 20:4 so extreme as to say those are condemned by God. No, what God says is, "Make no graven image that you then worship." In Exodus 25 he told the Israelites, "Put these statues on the Ark." They didn't worship the statues, which reminded the Israelites of God.

The verses can be put together, if you understand their proper meaning. If you take one verse alone, and then take off on a tangent, you will misunderstand what God is saying to his people. You have to take the whole together, and then you'll see that there is nothing wrong with making a statue or other graven image. What's wrong is worshipping a false god or worshipping that very statue. That's idolatry, and that's condemned.

BLACKBURN: I'm not going to ask you how many of you have bowed down before the Virgin Mary and prayed to her. I'm just going to tell you there are words in those commandments that say, "Thou shall not make unto you any graven images." God meant exactly that. Not make unto you any graven image. Something that you're going to look upon and think has got some kind of spiritual powers. That's totally anti-Scripture. And you'll find if you look in Romans 1 that that's exactly what people with the mentality of the religious have done. It says they started worshipping the creature rather than the Creator.

QUESTIONER: Mr. Blackburn, I wonder if you believe in the healing of the body, of going to the elders of the Church or others to be prayed over, perhaps with laying on of hands and that through God's power healing can come down. If you do believe in that for the body, why can't you believe in the healing of the soul through God's power by going to the priest to pray with you?

BLACKBURN: In James 5 we have what this lady was discussing, the scriptural admonition and the way to deal with people who are sick. The elders of the church pray over them, heal them, pray for them, so forth and so on. I have no problems with that whatsoever. That's scriptural as can be. The healing that this lady is talking about—correct me if I'm wrong—is referring to the Virgin Mary, being pure and whole.

VOICES: Forgiveness of sins.

BLACKBURN: Forgiveness of sin. Oh, the priest? Well, first of all, if he didn't die for my sins, he sure as heck can't forgive them. If we give this man the power to forgive as implied there, he also has the power to withhold. Now, with that power to withhold comes tremendous power. In all clear honesty, if I had the keys, I don't know if I wouldn't own the world also because human nature—the Bible tells us in Jeremiah, that the heart is deceitful above all things. God would never trust man, carnal man, with the right to deny or open up the gates of heaven to another man. That's where corruption comes in and has come in. You could sell that power. Look in Acts 8 at Simon the sorcerer. That's exactly what he wanted.

KEATING: I see some residual Catholicism here. Mr. Blackburn is supporting the basis for the sacrament of the anointing of the sick, in James 5, also known as the last rites. I'm glad to hear that. I see no problem at all in granting that God has given human beings his own powers to heal bodily and also given them power, his own power, to heal spiritually.

QUESTIONER: I address this question to Mr. Keating. Sir, you did mention earlier that Mary is sinless. How could you explain in Luke 1:47 when she said, "My spirit rejoices in God my Savior"? And Romans 3:23 would say, "For all have sinned and fall short of the glory of God"?

KEATING: Even Fundamentalists say that young children cannot sin. Thus what was being said there by Paul wasn't applied to all human beings. It wasn't applied to young children. They weren't mentioned by exception. Mary didn't have to be mentioned by exception either. We say Mary was immaculately conceived, that the stain of original sin was not on her soul as it was on our souls. Here's the difference. You have a pit. A man is going along, he falls in. You save him by pulling him out after he falls in. Another man comes along, and before he falls in you grab his sleeve to prevent him falling in. In each case, a man has been saved—one after the fact, the other by anticipation. Mary was saved from the stain of original sin by anticipation. The rest of us have been saved from the stain of original sin at baptism, after the fact. She is saved by Jesus Christ just as we are. It came at the moment of her conception; for us it comes some time later.

BLACKBURN: The words of our Lord Jesus Christ concerning the exalted position of his mother: "And it came to pass as he spake these things a certain woman of the company lifted up her voice and said unto him, 'Blessed is the womb that bore thee and the paps that thou has sucked.'" But he said, "Yea, rather blessed are they that hear the word of God and keep it." Do you understand that Mary was conceived in sin, her children were conceived in sin? If she had an immaculate conception then also Joseph was born without sin too. Then Joseph's children were born without sin and on and on it goes. You're missing the fulfillment of Scripture, and you are taking Christ out of the picture. Christ wasn't holy because he was born of a virgin. He was holy because he's God's Son.

MODERATOR: This will be our last question.

QUESTIONER: You mentioned earlier that Catholic doctrines actually started earlier than the third century. Now I agree. In fact, we find confession to a priest, the worship of the queen of heaven, and even God in the bread all in Babylon, which God harshly condemned throughout Jeremiah, in the Old Testament. So what's your response that God already condemned these practices, and now they are found in Roman Catholicism?

KEATING: You have the facts wrong. Some Unitarians claim, "Oh, the Babylonians taught three gods therefore they taught the Trinity and therefore it's not a Christian doctrine. No, the Babylonians never taught the Trinity. This is the alternative Fundamentalist history, the Babylonian one. The standard Fundamentalist history concerns the year 325. In this Babylonian alternative, everything came from Babylon. It's a wonderful theory. It's like some people said, "All the evil in the world comes from Jews who are bankers," but that's not factual. This Fundamentalist theory concerning Babylon is simply not historical, not factual.

BLACKBURN: There's a tremendous book out by [Alexander] Hislop called *The Two Babylons*. Read it for yourself, and you decide for yourself. It's the most exhaustive documented work. It's the driest material you'll ever read, but you'll just see her. She just sits right in the middle of it, the Catholic Church.

MODERATOR: Thank you gentlemen. We will now have a closing statement, first by Rev. Blackburn for fifteen minutes and then by Mr. Keating.

BLACKBURN: Now I'm going to read to you, and what I'm going to read to you is Catholic material—Catholic words, the Church's teachings, whatever else you want. I don't want to discolor this, and I'm not trying to fault this man, okay? But Mr. Keating said earlier that the Catholic Church is the only Church with unity. Now, this is an article out of the *Los Angeles Times*, and it says right here, "Gay Priests, a Dilemma for Catholics." And this gentleman in the article finally says, "I cannot personally hold the Church's teaching on homosexuality, teach it or preach about it, I have to be disobedient in that regard." We know that there are nuns and other women of the Church who are fighting for birth control. They're fighting for the priesthood. It's not a church in unity by any means.

But now, let me ask you something. What would it matter if Mary was a perpetual virgin? What effect would it have on the Scriptures? None whatsoever. She wasn't. But I want to show you that she's more than highly venerated, and I want to read from Pope Pius IX, who was pope from 1846 to 1878. Now, I'm just quoting, folks. Don't get mad at me. "God has committed to Mary the treasury of all good things in order that everyone may know that through her are obtained every hope, every grace, and all salvation, for this is his will that we obtain everything through Mary." Pope Leo XIII: "As no man goes to the Father except through his Mother." St. Alphonsus Liguori in the *Glories of Mary*: "Mary is called the Gate of Heaven because no one can enter that blessed kingdom without passing through her."

This deals with what the Church really believes about the Bible. And what I'm going to do is quote exactly what the Church says. I'm quoting it out of this book, which is the New American Bible Catholic edition. And it starts out right here. This is in the Dogmatic Constitution on Divine Revelation from Vatican II. And it says this. "Those divinely revealed realities which are contained and presented in Sacred Scripture have been committed to writing under the inspiration of the Holy Spirit." I agree with that. "For Holy Mother Church holds that the books of both the Old and the New Testament, in their entirety, with all their parts, are sacred because written under the inspiration of the Holy Spirit. They have God as their author." I agree with all that. "Therefore, since everything asserted by the inspired authors or sacred writers must be held to be asserted by the Holy Spirit, it follows that the books of Scripture must be acknowledged as teaching solidly, faithfully, and without error that truth which God wanted put into the sacred writings for the sake of our salvation." It quotes 2 Timothy 3:16-17, "All Scripture is given by inspiration of God."

Then it goes on. "The plan of salvation foretold by the sacred authors is found as the true word of God in the books of the Old Testament. These books, therefore, written under divine inspiration, remain of permanent value. God, the inspirer and author of both Testaments, wisely arranged that the New Testament be hidden in the Old Testament and the Old Testament be made manifest in the New." Tremendous words. It's true. "The Church has always and everywhere held and continues to hold that the four Gospels are of apostolic origin. Holy Mother Church has firmly and with absolute constancy held and continues to hold that the four Gospels faithfully hand on what Jesus Christ really did and taught until he was taken into heaven. Besides the four Gospels, the canon of the New Testament also contains the epistles of St. Paul and the other apostolic writings composed under the inspiration of the Holy Spirit by which, according to the wise plan of God, those matters which concern the Lord are confirmed."

Folks, I don't disagree with a word of that. Now, let me read you something else and see if you applaud. "In the congregations, mainly in the cities around the Mediterranean, they found scores of narratives about Jesus. The writers took these narratives and frequently remolded and refashioned them to bring out the lesson they wanted to teach. Moreover, some of these accounts may be adaptations of similar ones in the Old Testament. In the conflict stories of the Gospel, it is usually"—get this—"Jesus who is in conflict with his opponents, those Jews who did not believe in him." Was Jesus involved in these conversations? Did he answer exactly as related in the Bible?

Listen to these words. "It is not certain. Since we do not possess a biography of Jesus, it is difficult to know whether the words or sayings attributed to him are written exactly as he spoke them." Another question is, did Jesus sit on a hill and give the beatitudes? Now, listen to this. "The ancient tradition that the author of the Gospel of Matthew was the disciple and apostle of Jesus named Matthew is untenable. The unknown author, whom we shall continue to call Matthew for the sake of convenience—" blah, blah, blah.

Then we go into the Gospel of John. "Although tradition identified this person"—and Mr. Keating loves tradition—"the writer of the Gospel of John as John the son of Zebedee, Jesus' apostle, most modern scholars find that the evidence does not support this." But I just read that she has always held onto this and still does. Now, let's go on with this further. "Most scientists hold that the human species have developed somehow from lower kinds of life."

That's called evolution, for those who don't grasp it. "This knowledge helped Christians to re-think the how of God's creative activity and to understand that Genesis chapters 2 and 3 are not a lesson in anthropology but an allegory." Now that's what your church believes. And if that's what you want, great. That's strictly up to you. And if you believe that we evolved, well, that's too bad for you, because the Word of God stands firm today that he created us, and I don't have an ancestor that came from a monkey or an elephant or anything else, and I'm sorry about you. Now, if you want to honor the Virgin Mary, just go right ahead.

Now, I just want you to know this. I believe and I know that the truth was presented to you today, and Jesus said, "Do you hate me because I've told you the truth? Why are you trying to kill me?" And they didn't know what to do. But that's what they were trying to do because he told them the truth. And he said, "He that rejecteth my words and receive not me has one that judgeth him. My words in the last days will be used to judge him." You've heard enough today to know the truth. Now, you can keep your mind closed, you can refuse to look this up and study it out for yourself, you can trust in Mr. Keating, you can trust in your priest, you can trust in the Church, that Mary was assumed up into heaven and that she made this vow that is non-scriptural. You can have all of these if you want, but I want you to understand you've made a god out of Mary.

In chapter nine of his book, pages 121 through 125, Mr. Keating deals with inspiration of the Bible. We can go back through prophetical observations or fulfillments, archeological facts, scientific data, historical facts, and we can prove that the Scriptures are true. When they dug up the Dead Sea Scrolls, they found out that the book of Isaiah that they found, except for, I believe, three punctuation marks, was identical to the book of Isaiah in the King James Bible. We can go through and validate these things. If I had, for instance, an orange here in my hand, I'd say, "this orange speaks for itself, it's an orange." We have the taste of the orange, the color of the orange, the texture of the skin. The orange has evidences within itself that it is an orange. If it said I'm a lemon, we could say, "Oh, no you're not." We can prove it. The Bible has evidences to support itself, that it is what it says it is, the inspired word of God, the infallible word of God. Mr. Keating says, "No, no, no, we do the same thing as you do, to certain extents, but then we stop and we say that the Church says it's the inspired word of God. And now that the Church has said it, you can use it. But until the Church says it's the inspired word of God, it's not inspired." Folks, that's like saying this orange here is an orange, and you know it, but you cannot believe it is an orange until I tell you that it is an orange. You can't weigh the evidences within it yourself. You have to accept my word.

Now, let me show you what they've done with that. First of all, God said, "All Scripture is given by inspiration of God." God said it's inspired. Mr. Keating says the Church says it's inspired. Don't believe God, believe the Church. Jesus said, "I am the way, the truth, and the life." The Church says, "No, you can only attain salvation through me!" So God's out, and the Church is in. Jesus is out, and the Church is in. The Bible says that it is the Holy Spirit that guides us and teaches us into all truth. They say, no, the Church does it. So now they've kicked out God, they've kicked out Jesus, and they've kicked out the Holy Spirit. The Trinity doesn't remain, but who does? Mary?

Let me show you how great Mary is, while I've still got time here. It tells us this in a 1919 Carmelite devotion to the Virgin Mary. It says right here about their scapular that if you are wearing this little scapular with a picture of Mary on it, she'll pull you out of purgatory on the first Saturday after you die. Isn't that something? It's totally unreal. I can't believe this. It says, "To whom should they turn but to Mary who never forsakes her children?" I got news for you. Mary may be your mother, she's not mine. Let me give you one other thing. This is real bad, I know, but I'm kind of a bad guy. When you call Mary the Mother of God, the daughter of the Son, that makes an incestuous relationship. The Mother of God, the daughter of the Father. That's an incestuous relationship. When you call her the Queen of Heaven, she can't be the Queen unless she's married to the King. And there is another incestuous relationship because Jesus is the King. Although you cannot find this in the Scripture, I know the holy Church says it's so, so it must be so. I'll tell you what I'll do. I'll take the book, you take the Church.

KEATING: I agree that the truth was presented to you this afternoon, and I'll continue to present it. The Catholic interpretation of the Bible can be found all the way back historically. Fundamentalist interpretations are, historically speaking, novelties. They only go back a few centuries at best. Look at such things as the Bible-alone theory, entirely unknown before the Reformation. The absolute assurance of salvation, entirely unknown before that point. Adult-only baptism, some ways into the Reformation. The rapture, even newer than that, from nineteenth-century dispensationalism. The notion that the Second Coming of our Lord is imminent, within our own lifetimes, and that we can figure out the dates. All inventions.

You might have heard about a man named Edgar Whisenant who published a book called *88 Reasons Why the Rapture Will Be in 1988.* He went through, in a Fundamentalist fashion, the books that have prophecy in them, and he concluded that the rapture would occur during Rosh Hashanah in September of that year. Well, September came and went. Whisenant, who sold four million copies of his book, said, "I made a mistake. I forgot there was no year zero. The rapture will occur in September 1989 instead." September 1989 came and went. Our Lord said, "You know neither the day nor the hour." Whisenant said, "Yes, but you can know the week and the month." That kind of playing with Scripture is unhistorical, it's contrary to the Christian faith, and it's indicative of Fundamentalism.

Which is the true Church? There can be only one because Jesus established only one. That Church is historically identical with the Catholic Church, which has unity of doctrine. It always has taught the same. Have there been individual Catholics who have been in error? Yes, in the past and today. There are Catholics who say, "Oh, I don't believe in the Resurrection," but the Church does not agree with them. There are Catholics who say, "Oh, I don't believe in the Redemption," but the Church does not teach that. The Church always has taught the same. Individual Christians will come and will go, will err. The Church does not err. There is complete conformity with biblical teaching in what the Catholic Church teaches. There are unconformities in Fundamentalism.

You can ignore facts. I brought up many of them today, such as what the early Christians wrote. You can ignore facts, but you can't refute them. There has been no effort made by Mr. Blackburn to refute the facts that show the early Christians, and Christians throughout the centuries, believed as the Catholic Church still teaches. "Who hears you, hears me," said Jesus, and he said that to the apostles. "Who hears you, hears me." There are some people who refused to hear Jesus, the apostles, and their successors. They refuse to hear Jesus and instead, as Peter warns, twist Scripture to their own destruction. They overlook or even pervert sections of Scripture when those sections don't match their pet theories or inventions.

Go to a Fundamentalist church and sit in on the services. Do it consistently, for a period of time. See what is preached about. Only parts of the Bible. Many parts are skipped over. In the Catholic Church, in the course of the three-year cycle of readings, you hear almost the entire New Testament read out. We accept it all. You don't find that in Fundamentalist churches.

Something you will not find any preaching about is the latter part of John 6. Do you remember what happens in John 6? In the beginning is a multiplication of fishes and loaves for the five thousand. Jesus miraculously provides earthly food for his people. Then he says, "Now I promise you that you will be getting, miraculously, spiritual food." He says, "If there is to be life within you, you must eat my flesh and drink my blood." What does the crowd say? First the Jews on the periphery say, "How can this man give us his flesh to eat?" They take him literally, not figuratively, not metaphorically. What does Jesus not do? He does not say, "No, you misunderstand, I'm just talking symbolically." In other cases, when Jesus was talking to the crowds, they misunderstood the full import. Even the apostles often misunderstood. So, he took the apostles aside later and said, "This is what I meant." He does not do that here. What does he do instead? Instead of saying, "You misunderstood me, I was speaking symbolically," he repeats himself: "You must eat my flesh and drink my blood."

Then what happens? Some of his disciples, people who had accepted everything he had taught up to this point, say, "This is a hard saying, who can accept it?" And what are we told? That they walked with him no more. This is the only place in the New Testament where anybody leaves Jesus for doctrinal reasons. It was over the Real Presence of Jesus in the Eucharist. What did Jesus not do? He did not correct them. He again said, "You must eat my flesh and drink my blood." He let his own followers depart. And who also did not accept Jesus at his word? Look at John 6:64; it was Judas.

This is where Judas fell. He would not accept this great central truth of the Real Presence of Jesus, under the appearances of bread and wine. Read chapter 6 for yourself. Here Judas falls away. Unlike the other disciples who left, he didn't actually leave in body, but he left in mind and in heart. Later on we're told he was a thief, stealing from the common purse, but that's not what turned him against Jesus. This was the point, his refusal to accept an explicit teaching of Jesus, one that Jesus continued to repeat.

Many Fundamentalists will say Jesus is talking symbolically when he refers to this truth as being "spirit and light." If anyone tells you that, have him show you elsewhere in the New Testament where the word "spirit" is used for symbolic teaching. No place. What Jesus is saying is that this is a high doctrine which you will not accept unless you are a true follower of his. If you are not a true spiritual follower, you will reject the Real Presence of Jesus in the Eucharist. That's what happened to Judas.

We're very blessed as Christians with having an opportunity to accept Jesus fully in all his words. We have no need to pick and choose. We follow the Church that he set up in Matthew 16:18 and follow those constant teachings which the Church has given. But some will not do so. How are we to decide, when so many claims are made? "I am for Christ," they said. "I am for Paul, I am for Apollo." Who taught truly? Scripture gives us many ways to discern.

There is one that I think might be especially appropriate today: to discern which is *not* the true way. And it is this: bitterness is not one of the fruits of the Holy Spirit. It does no good to say this is righteous anger. That's not what bitterness is. Bitterness is an indication that the soul needs reformation. I call upon all of you to go home today, open your Bibles, and read through the sixth chapter of John's Gospel. Pray to the Holy Spirit that he will enlighten you as to the true meaning. If you do that, you will understand why Jesus is truly, corporally present in the Eucharist, and you will begin to see, if this applies to you, a lessening of bitterness against the Church which maybe once you embraced, but now, like a rejected lover, you have cast off. Thank you very much.

MODERATOR: Ladies and gentlemen, on behalf of both of our participants, we wish to thank you all for being here. You've been a gracious audience. Thank you very much. Let's hear it once again for our debaters.

Thank You!

I hope you found this little book useful or entertaining—preferably both! If you did, please consider leaving an honest review at Amazon. It is through reviews that writers find most of their new readers.

If you have feedback about the book, I'd like to have it. You can write to me at Karl@KarlKeating.com.

The Books in This Series

The Debating Catholicism Series consists of four short books and an omnibus volume. They are:

Book 1: *The Bible Battle* (Karl Keating vs. Peter S. Ruckman)

Book 2: *High Desert Showdown* (Karl Keating vs. Jim Blackburn)

Book 3: *Tracking Down the True Church* (Karl Keating vs. Jose Ventilacion)

Book 4: *Face Off with an Ex-Priest* (Karl Keating vs. Bartholomew F. Brewer)

Omnibus Volume: *Debating Catholicism* (includes all four books above)

Other Books by Karl Keating

Apologetics the English Way

Can a reasonable case be made for Catholicism? Maybe even a compelling case? Or does the Catholic argument falter? Does it wilt before critiques from top-notch opponents? Judge for yourself. You don't have to be Catholic or even religious to relish the intellectual sparring that goes on in these pages.

Here is high-level controversial writing, culled from Karl Keating's favorite books. Each selection is a forceful exposition of Catholic truth. Most are from the 1930s, all come from English Catholics, and all are aimed at a single antagonist, with the public invited to look over the writer's shoulder. The reader can view the weaknesses and occasional mistakes even of his own champion.

These pages are filled with vivid personalities. These were men who knew the Catholic faith and could explain it to others. The individuals against whom they wrote may not have been converted—one or two were, in the long run—but any number of readers of these little-known masterpieces must have found their faith bolstered and their doubts assuaged. The issues covered in these exchanges are still discussed today—but probably nowhere in as glorious a style as here.

The New Geocentrists

Were Copernicus, Galileo, and Kepler wrong? Does Earth orbit the Sun, or does the Sun orbit Earth? For centuries, everyone thought the science was settled, but today the accepted cosmology is being challenged by writers, speakers, and movie producers who insist that science took a wrong turn in the seventeenth century. These new geocentrists claim not only that Earth is the center of our planetary system but that Earth is motionless at the very center of the universe.

They insist they have the science to back up their claims, which they buttress with evidence from the Bible and Church documents. But do they have a case? How solid is their reasoning, and how trustworthy are they as interpreters of science and theology?

The New Geocentrists examines the backgrounds, personalities, and arguments of the people involved in what they believe is a revolutionary movement, one that will overthrow the existing cosmological order and, as a consequence, change everyone's perception of the status of mankind.

No Apology

Karl Keating has been a Catholic apologist for nearly four decades. In these pages he shares some of his own experiences and some stories from times past. He writes about how to do apologetics and how not to. He defends the very idea of apologetics against a theologian who thinks apologetics is passé. He looks at how the faith is promoted through beauty and through suffering. He takes you from his own backyard to such distant times and places as fifth-century Jerusalem and sixteenth-century Japan.

Anti-Catholic Junk Food

You are what you eat. That is as true of the mind as of the body. Eat enough greasy food, and your silhouette will betray your culinary preferences. Give credence to enough greasy ideas, and your mind will be as flabby as your waistline. This book looks at eight examples of religious junk food, things that have come across Karl Keating's desk during his career as a Catholic apologist. You likely will find these morsels unconvincing and unpalatable, as you should. The problem is that plenty of people—including people on your block—consider such stuff to be intellectual high cuisine.

Jeremiah's Lament

For many, the best way to reach an understanding of the Catholic Church is to see how other people misunderstand it. This book is full of misunderstandings.

The people quoted in these pages came to their confusions in various ways. Sometimes it was by reading the wrong books or by failing to read the right books. Sometimes it was a matter of heredity, with prejudices passed down from father to son and from mother to daughter. At other times errors were imbibed at the foot of the pulpit, in the university lecture hall, or from door-to-door missionaries.

Whatever their origin, misunderstandings are misunderstandings. They should be recognized for what they are and set aside, even if that means a break from personal habit or family tradition. More than a century ago, Pope Leo XIII noted that there is nothing so salutary as to understand the world as it really is. That is true particularly of the Church that Christ established because to misunderstand her is to misunderstand him.

How to Fail at Hiking Mt. Whitney

Often, the best way to succeed at something is to learn how to fail at it—and then to avoid the things that lead to failure. There are books that tell you how to succeed at hiking Mt. Whitney. This book helps you *not* to fail by showing you what *not* to do, from the moment you start planning your trip to the moment you reach the summit.

You learn what gear not to buy and not to take, how to maximize your chances of getting a hiking permit (don't apply for the wrong days of the week!), how to prepare yourself physically without over-preparing, how to avoid being laid low by altitude or weather problems, how not to take too much food or water—or too little. You even discover how to shave a mile off the trip by using little-known shortcuts that can make the difference between reaching the summit and reaching exhaustion.

Most people who depart the Mt. Whitney trailhead fail to reach the top. Some fail because of things entirely beyond their control, but many fail because of insufficient preparation, false expectations, and basic errors of judgment. Their mistakes can come at the beginning (such as failing to get a hiking permit), during the preparation stage (such as being induced to buy "bombproof" gear), or during the hike (such as not heeding bodily warning signs).

Through engaging stories of his own and others' failures, Karl Keating shows you how to fail—and therefore how to succeed—at hiking the tallest peak in the 48 contiguous states.

About Karl Keating

Karl Keating holds advanced degrees in theology and law (University of San Diego) plus an honorary doctor of laws degree (Ave Maria University). He founded Catholic Answers, the English-speaking world's largest lay-run Catholic apologetics organization. His best-known books are *Catholicism and Fundamentalism* (nearly a quarter-million paperback copies sold) and *What Catholics Really Believe* (about half that many sold). His avocations include hiking, studying languages, and playing the baroque mandolino. He lives in San Diego. You can follow him at his author website and on Facebook:

KarlKeating.com
Facebook.com/KarlKeatingBooks

www.ingramcontent.com/pod-product-compliance
Lightning Source LLC
Chambersburg PA
CBHW060717030426
42337CB00017B/2908